中国的女皇帝武则天
Empress of China
WU ZE TIAN

编文：姜成安　　**Written by : Jiang, Cheng An**
绘画：徐德元　　**Illustrated by : Xu, De Yuan**

胜利出版社

Victory Press

Victory Press
543 Lighthouse Avenue, Monterey, CA 93940
(831) 883-1725 / fax (831) 883-8710

ISBN: 1-878217-32-1   trade   1-878217-31-3   paper

Printed in Hong Kong

Library of Congress Cataloging-in-Publication Data

Chiang, Ch'eng-an.
       Empress of China, Wu Ze Tian / written by Jiang Cheng An ;
illustrated by Xu De Yuan = [Chung-kuo ti nu huang ti Wu Tse-t' ien]
/ pien wen Chiang Ch'eng-an ; hui hua Hsu Te-yuan.
              p.   cm.
       Parallel title in Chinese characters.
       English and Chinese.
       Summary: Tells the story of Wu Ze Tian, a palace attendant who
became China's only female emperor and brought prosperity and
cultural growth to China during the T'ang dynasty.
       ISBN 1-878217-32-1. - - ISBN 1-878217-31-3 (pbk.)
       1. Wu hou, Empress of China, 624-705--Juvenile literature.
2. Empresses—China—Biography--Jjuvenile literature. [1. Wu hou,
Empress of China, 624-705. 2. Kings, queens, rulers, etc.
3. China—History--T'ang dynasty, 618-907. 4. Women--Biography.
5. Chinese language materials--Bilingual.]   I. Xu De Yuan, ill.
II. Title.
DS749.42.W8C48   1998
951' .017'092--dc21   98-24319
[b]   CIP
                                             AC

English by Eileen Hu

唐太宗统治的唐朝，是中国历史上的黄金时代。那时艺术、诗歌、宗教都很繁荣。中国的势力北至蒙古，南达越南，东至中亚。

Emperor Tang Tai Zong ruled China during the Tang Dynasty, a golden age in China's history. During this time art, poetry, and religion flourished. China's influence spread from Mongolia in the north to Vietnam in the south and Central Asia in the east.

唐太宗有许多宫女，他最宠爱的宫女之一就是武媚娘。她是一个活泼聪明的女孩，出生于一个富有的木材商人家庭，十四岁就被选入宫中。

Emperor Tang Tai Zong had many attendants. One of his favorites was the beautiful Wu Mei Niang. She was a lively and intelligent girl from a wealthy lumber merchant family. She was choosen to live at the imperial palace at fourteen.

太宗死后，媚娘便不能留在宫中了。按照古老的宫规，她被送入感业寺当尼姑。

When Emperor Tang Tai Zong died, Wu Mei Niang could no longer remain in the imperial palace. According to ancient tradition, she was sent to Gan Ye Buddhist Temple to live.

寺庙里的生活很辛苦。武媚娘每天早晨在佛像前烧香，白天要挑水、砍柴、烧饭及做清洁的工作，晚上还要念经。

Life at the temple was hard. Early every morning Wu Mei Niang burned incense on the alter and she chanted sutras late into the evening. During the day, she carried water from the river for cleaning, and chopped fire wood for cooking.

与此同时，太宗的儿子唐高宗登上了皇帝的宝座。一天，他到感业寺去烧香。

Meanwhile, the Emperor's son Tang Gao Zong became the new Emperor of China. One day the new Emperor entered Gan Ye Temple to burn incense.

武媚娘以一个娇美的微笑接近新皇帝。新皇帝无法抵御她的魅力，终于将她带回到长安的皇宫。

Wu Mei Niang approached the new Emperor with a beautiful smile. The new Emperor could not resist her charm. Wu Mei Niang was able to convince him to take her back to the imperial palace in Chang An.

　　回宫后，媚娘被封为妃子，成了新皇帝的一个妻子。她总是很爱打听，宫中的一切事情她都想知道。为此，她和宫中各处的宫女交好，她们向她透露各种信息。

Wu Mei Niang entered the palace as a concubine, one of many wives to the new Emperor. Always curious, she wanted to know what was happening in other parts of the palace. In order to do this, she made friends with the servants who were in charge of various parts of the palace. These servants would reveal information to her.

有宫女告诉武媚娘王皇后的秘密，皇后非常妒忌媚娘的美貌和聪颖。她因皇帝过于宠幸媚娘而烦恼。她的妒火使她正密谋杀害媚娘。

A few of these servants told Wu Mei Niang a secret about Empress Wang，the official wife of the Emperor. Empress Wang was very jealous of Wu Mei Niang's beauty and intelligence. She was upset because the Emperor spent too much time with Wu Mei Niang. The Empress was so jealous she was plotting to kill Wu Mei Niang.

媚娘为自己的性命担忧，她焦急地思索着："她是皇后，而我只是一个嫔妃。我怎样才能保全自己的性命呢？"突然，她心生一计，但她必须作出一个巨大的牺牲才能实现她的计划。于是，她杀掉自己亲生的女婴，然后把责任推到王皇后身上。

Mei Niang feared for her life. She anxiously thought to herself, "What can I do to save myself? She is the Empress and I am only a concubine." Suddenly, an idea came to Wu Mei Niang, but she would have to make a big sacrifice in order for the plan to succeed. So, she killed her own baby daughter, but blamed Empress Wang for the death of the infant.

高宗得知王皇后害死了他的女儿，就将其废黜并逐出皇宫。然后，举行了一个盛大的仪式，在锣鼓声中立武媚娘为皇后，并赐名武则天。

When the Emperor heard the news that his wife Empress Wang had murdered his daughter, he removed her title as Empress and banished her from the palace. Then, in a huge ceremony with drums and cymbals he raised Wu Mei Niang to the position of Empress of China, giving her the official title Wu Ze Tian.

高宗患病后，武则天便开始从幕后统治中国了。每当患病的高宗临朝，武则天便坐在屏风后倾听。通过这种方式，她获得了足够的信息以给高宗的决策提出建议。

When the Emperor became ill, Wu Ze Tian started to rule China from behind the scenes. Whenever the ill Emperor held Court, Wu Ze Tian would sit behind a screen and listen to the proceedings. In this way she was able to gather enough information to advise the Emperor.

　　武则天深知自己学业浅，缺乏经验，因此她挑选了一大批有才华的大臣来帮助自己辅佐患病的高宗。

She was aware of her lack of education and lack of experience, so she selected many talented ministers and officials to help her advise the ill Emperor.

在高宗患病期间，武则天倡导了许多利民措施，诸如军队闲暇时种地及大兴水利等。

During the Emperor's illness, Wu Ze Tian also suggested many measures that would benefit the common people. For example, soldiers were to grow crops in their spare time. Wu Ze Tian also started many irrigation projects.

　　高宗对武则天权力的增大日益恐慌，这对他不利。于是，他册立皇子李弘为太子。李弘是武则天的长子。

The ill Emperor Tang Gao Zong became increasingly alarmed at Wu Ze Tian's growing power. This was not good for him. Therefore，he named his son Li Hong as crown prince. Li Hong was the first-born son of Wu Ze Tian.

已经尝到权力甜头的武则天一心想继续统治国家。因此，她一旦发现儿子不听从她时，便毫不犹豫地将他废黜，继而用毒酒将他杀害。

But Wu Ze Tian already had a taste of power and she wanted to keep ruling. When her son Li Hong was disrespectful to her, she had him removed from his position as crown prince. Later, she had him killed with poisoned alcohol.

17

公元683年唐高宗死后，时年五十九岁的武则天成为皇太后，并以她三子、四子的名义统治国家。

When Emperor Tang Gao Zong died in the year 683 AD，Wu Ze Tian was fifty-nine. She became Empress Dowager and ruled in the name of her third and fourth sons.

大臣徐敬业对武则天运用权术使儿子成为傀儡自己行统治天下之实的行为深感不满。

A minister named Xu Jing Ye was dissatisfied with Wu Ze Tian's use of power，especially with the way she used her sons as puppets while she actually governed China herself.

于是他纠集数十万士卒，起兵反对武则天。

Xu Jing Ye gathered hundreds of thousands of soldiers and horses and started a revolt against Wu Ze Tian.

尽管他们进攻了皇宫，但武则天在不到四十天里就平息了叛乱。此外，她还平息了其他反对她的叛乱。

Although they attacked the palace, Wu Ze Tian quelled the revolt in less than 40 days. In addition, she was able to suppress other revolts against her.

在她六十七岁那年，武则天自立为皇帝，成为中国五千余年历史上的唯一的女皇帝。

Wu Ze Tian then proclaimed herself Emperor of China at age 67. She is the only female emperor in more than 5,000 years of China's history.

因为武则天注意倾听民众的
呼声并采纳好的建议，所以，朝中
贤能的文官和善战的武将众多。

Because Wu Ze Tian respected
people's advice and she followed
it, her court was full of talented
officials and knowledgeable mili-
tary generals.

特别是，武则天制定的政策之一是准许平民举报贪官、奸商和其他有权势的人物。

In particular, one of Wu Ze Tian's policies allowed commoners to inform the palace of corrupt officials, merchants, or other powerful people.

　　士农兵商，不管地位高低，均可直接向朝廷检举揭发某人的恶行。

Regardless of their position, farmers, merchants, soldiers, or scholars could go directly to the imperial court to report negative information about someone.

Wu Ze Tian did not allow family ties to influence her political decisions. Wu Ze Tian appointed her nephew Wu Cheng Si to be prime minister. A few years later, an official named Li warned her, "Wu Cheng Si's power is growing too fast. He may later attempt to take over the throne."

武则天不允许由于亲属关系而影响她自己的集权统治。有一位姓李的大臣劝诫她道："你的侄子武承嗣当了宰相这几年权力飞快增长，有朝一日很可能篡夺帝位。"

于是，武则天马上免除了她侄子的宰相职务。武承嗣因此发出怨言，但武则天斥责道："李大臣很能干。他替我效力，你怎能和他相比！"

Wu Ze Tian then removed her nephew from office. When he complained, she stated, "Official Li is very capable. He works very hard for me. How can you compare?"

有一次，武则天筹划建造一尊宏大的佛像，宰相反对说："如今的寺庙比皇宫华丽。僧尼们向平民百姓索取大量布施。"

Once Wu Ze Tian planned to build a splendid Buddhist statue by taking daily donations from Buddhist temples. However, her prime minister was against the project. He said, "Today's Buddhist temples are more elaborate than the palace. Monks and nuns demand many donations from the commoners."

"一旦平民百姓没饭吃时，他们自己也就会变成和尚和尼姑了。"他接着说道："如此下去，耕田的人就会越来越少，由种田人养活的僧尼就会越来越多。这怎能有利于国家呢？"

"When the commoners don't have enough to eat, they themselves become monks and nuns," her minister continued. "In this way, there will be fewer and fewer people farming and more and more monks and nuns who will have to be supported by the farmers. How can this help China?"

武则天觉得宰相说得有道
理，建造佛像的事便作罢了。
**Wu Ze Tian agreed that her
prime minister was correct. She
stopped the work on the Buddhist
statue.**

公元705年，武则天辞世，终年八十二岁。她和她的丈夫唐高宗合葬于皇陵。

Wu Ze Tian died in the year 705 AD at the age of 82. She was buried with her husband Emperor Tang Gao Zong in the imperial mausoleum.

武则天统治中国时期，政治安定，人口增多，粮食充足，佛教风行全国，丝织业兴旺发达。

While Wu Ze Tian ruled China，the government was stable，the population increased，food was plentiful，Buddhism spread throughout the country，and the silk industry flourished.